Starting off with
Multiplying
and Dividing

Written by Peter Patilla

Illustrations by Liz Pichon

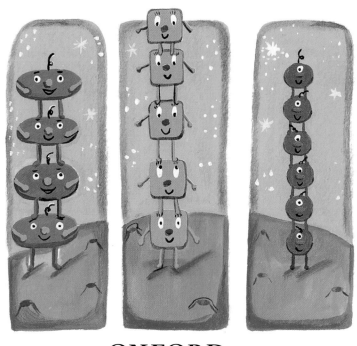

OXFORD
UNIVERSITY PRESS

OXFORD
UNIVERSITY PRESS

Great Clarendon Street, Oxford OX2 6DP

Oxford University Press is a department of the University of Oxford.
It furthers the University's objective of excellence in research, scholarship,
and education by publishing worldwide in

Oxford New York

Athens Auckland Bangkok Bogotá Buenos Aires Cape Town
Chennai Dar es Salaam Delhi Florence Hong Kong Istanbul Karachi
Kolkata Kuala Lumpur Madrid Melbourne Mexico City Mumbai
Nairobi Paris São Paulo Singapore Taipei Tokyo Toronto Warsaw

with associated companies in Berlin Ibadan

Oxford is a registered trade mark of Oxford University Press
in the UK and in certain other countries

British Library Cataloguing in Publication Data available

H/b ISBN 0–19–910795–5
P/b ISBN 0–19–910796–3

1 3 5 7 9 10 8 6 4 2

Designed and Typeset by Perry Tate Design
Printed in Hong Kong

My name is

The   Butlers ♡

....

Notes for parents and teachers

This book develops early concepts of *multiplying and dividing* for adults and children to enjoy and share together. It has been carefully written to introduce the key words and ideas related to *multiplying and dividing* which children will meet in their first couple of years in school.

Throughout the book you will see **Word Banks** which contain the new mathematical words introduced for each concept. All the words from the word bank are gathered together at the back of the book. You can use the word banks with your child in several ways:

- See which of the words are recognized through games such as *I spy. I spy the word sharing – can you find it? I spy a word beginning with m – where is it?*
- Choose a word and ask your child to find it in the book.
- Let your child choose a word from the word bank at the back of the book, and say something about it.

Look for other opportunities in everyday life to use the ideas and vocabulary introduced in this book. Compare and talk about 'lots of' and 'sharing' such as: how many things there are in a twin-pack, cutting a cake in half, sharing sweets out fairly. Ensure that children realize that multiplying and dividing is easy and, most importantly, fun.

Doubles

When something is doubled, there will be two times as many.

Doubles are two of anything.

double six

double roll

Twins are doubles.

twins

twin-pack

When you double things, there will be twice as many.

twice as many

What is the total of these doubles?

How many aliens would there be if you doubled them?

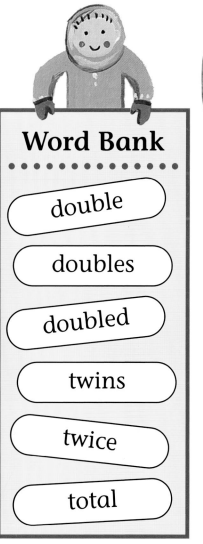

Word Bank

- double
- doubles
- doubled
- twins
- twice
- total

Multiplying

When you are multiplying you add lots of the same number together.

There will be four lots of two legs on these aliens.

That is 2 + 2 + 2 + 2 = 8.
You are multiplying 2 by 4.

You can write this using the multiplication sign ×.

$2 × 4 = 8$

There will be five lots of four legs on these aliens.

That is 4 + 4 + 4 + 4 + 4 = 20.
You are multiplying 4 by 5.

$4 × 5 = 20$

How many eyes are there in each group of aliens?

This alien has ten arms.
How many arms will be on five aliens?

Word Bank

multiplying

multiplication

lots of

add

same

how many?

Jumping along and multiplying

We can use a number track to help with multiplying.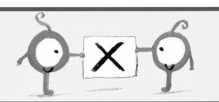

Multiplying is the same as adding the same number lots of times.

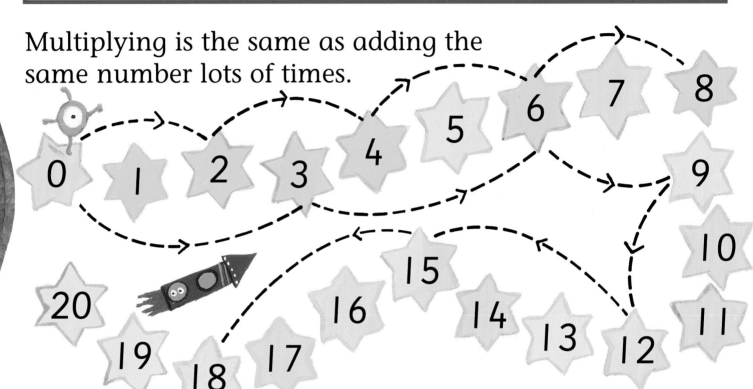

Start on zero.
Make four hops of 2.
You land on 8.
Add 2 four times and you get 8.
2 multiplied by 4 equals 8.

$$2 \times 4 = 8$$

Start on zero.
Make six hops of 3.
You land on 18.
Add 3 six times and you get 18.
3 multiplied by 6 equals 18.

$$3 \times 6 = 18$$

Use the number track to help you with these multiplications.

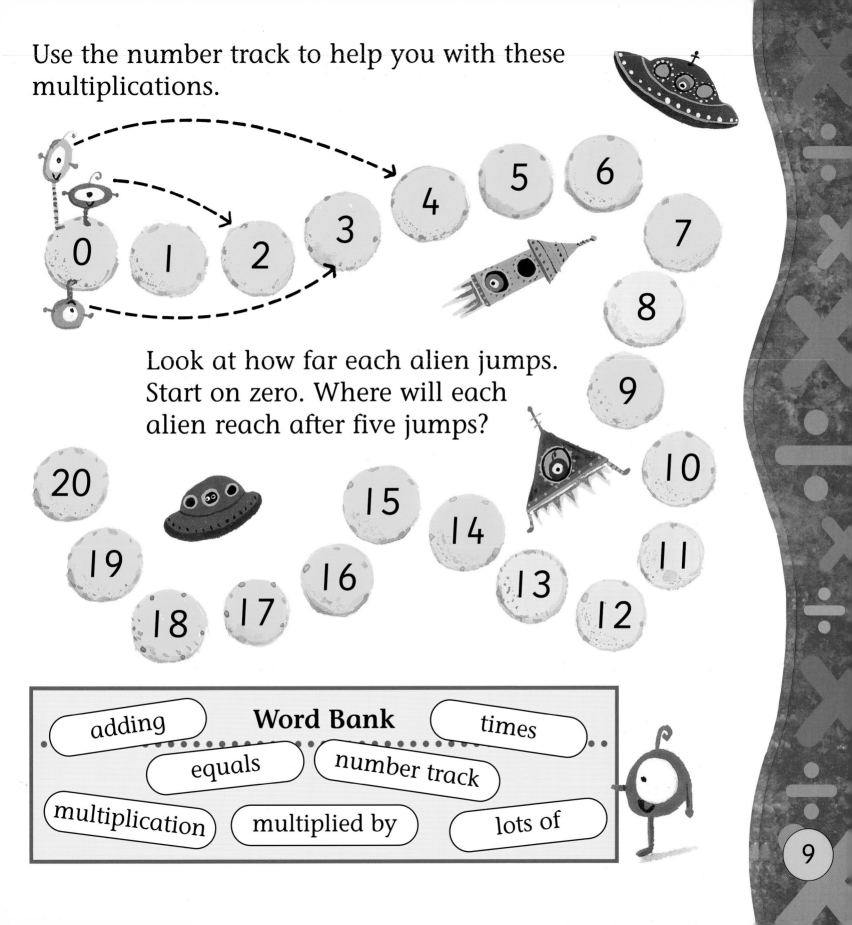

Look at how far each alien jumps. Start on zero. Where will each alien reach after five jumps?

Word Bank

adding
times
equals
number track
multiplication
multiplied by
lots of

Dividing in half

When you divide something in half there will be two pieces.
Each piece should be the same size.

These have all been divided in half.

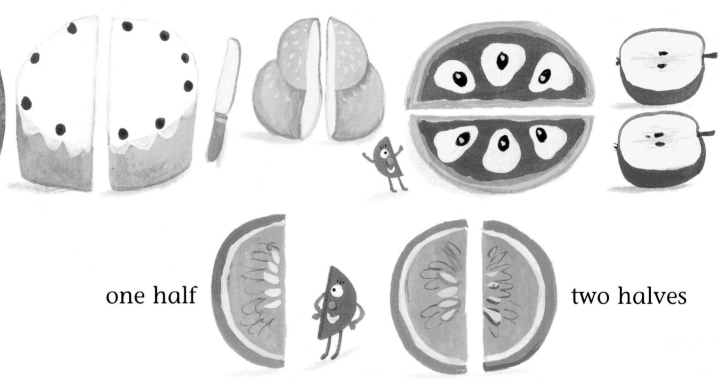

one half   two halves

You can divide a thing in half in different ways.

You can divide all kinds of things in half.

half a glass full

Which of these glasses are half full? Which of the glasses are more than half full?

Word Bank

- half
- halves
- divide
- more than
- less than
- same size

Which of these pizza slices are halves? Which of the slices are less than half?

Halving

When you halve anything there will be two parts. Each part should be equal.

6 halved

6 not halved

The alien is halving the chocolate bar.
Each alien will get 6 pieces each.

12

Halve the number of creatures in each group.
How many will there be in each half?

Here are some halves.
How many were there to start with?

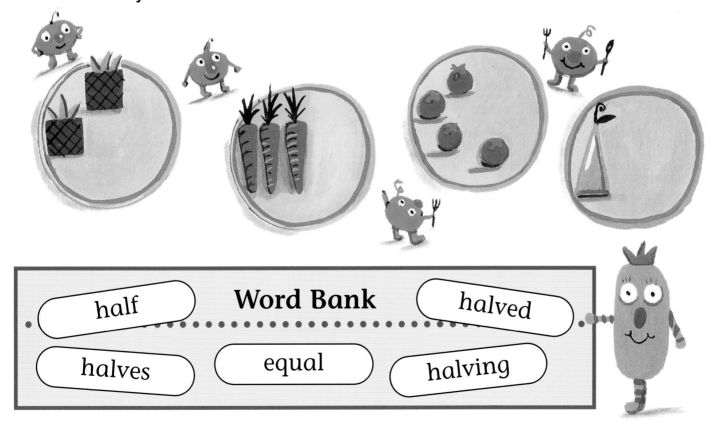

Word Bank

half   halved

halves   equal   halving

Quarters

When you divide things into quarters there will be four parts. Each part will be the same size.

These have all been divided into quarters.

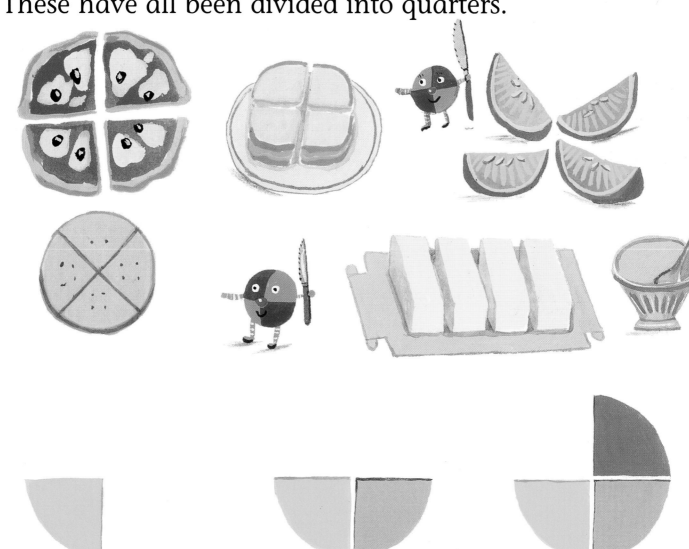

one quarter   two quarters   three quarters

Which of these have been cut into quarters?

Which of these slices is a quarter?
Which are larger than a quarter?
Which is smaller than a quarter?

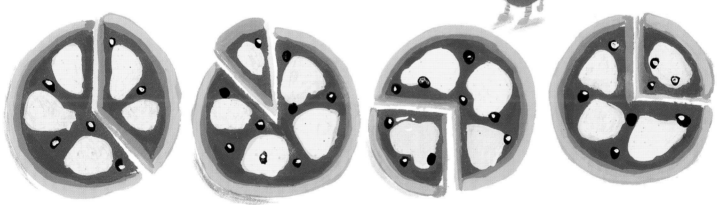

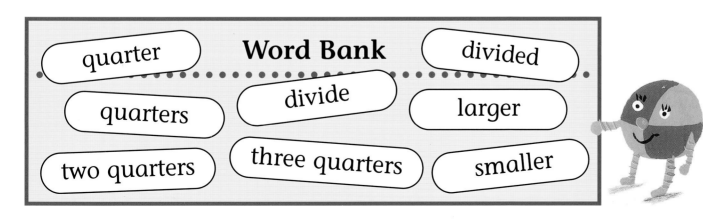

Word Bank

quarter   divided

quarters   divide   larger

two quarters   three quarters   smaller

Whole

A whole has no part missing.

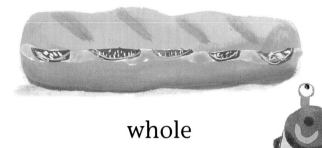

whole

not whole

Something whole can be divided into equal parts.

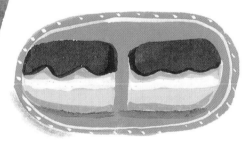

a whole divided
into halves

a whole divided
into thirds

a whole divided
into quarters

The parts are called
fractions.
Here are two fractions.

halves

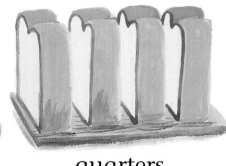

quarters

Look at these fractions.
Put the fractions together to make wholes.

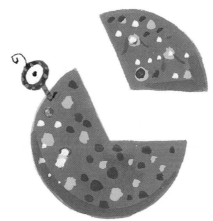

Which of these sandwiches have been divided fairly?

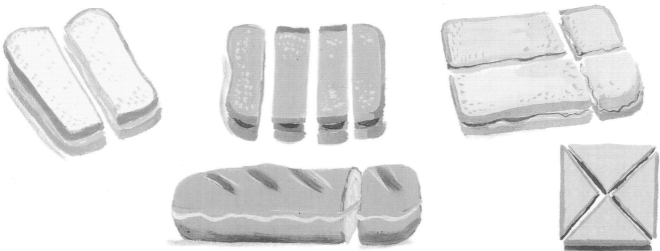

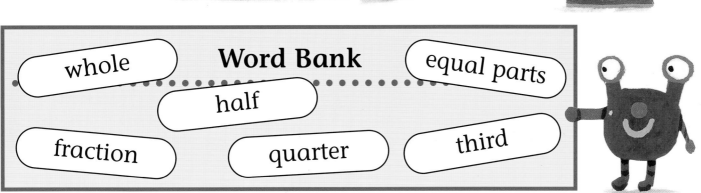

Word Bank

whole

equal parts

half

fraction

quarter

third

Sharing

When you share, each part must be the same. Dividing and sharing are the same thing.
The sign for dividing and sharing is ÷.

Here are 12 flowers shared in different ways.

12 divided into two

12 divided into three

12 divided into four

| 12 ÷ 2 |

| 12 ÷ 3 |

| 12 ÷ 4 |

Here is 9 shared by 3.

| 9 ÷ 3 |

Divide each of these by 2.

Share these between the bears.
How many will each get?

Word Bank

share   same

dividing   shared by

sharing   divided   different

Remainders

Sometimes when you share things fairly there is some left over.
Any left over is called the remainder.

10 shared between three leaves a remainder of 1.

10 divided by 3 equals 3 remainder 1

$$10 \div 3 = 3 \quad \text{remainder} \quad 1$$

There are 2 fours in 10 and a remainder of 2.

10 divided by 4 equals 2 remainder 2

$$10 \div 4 = 2 \quad \text{remainder} \quad 2$$

Divide each of these sets by 3.
What will be the remainder?

Share these between the aliens.
How many will each get? What will the remainder be?

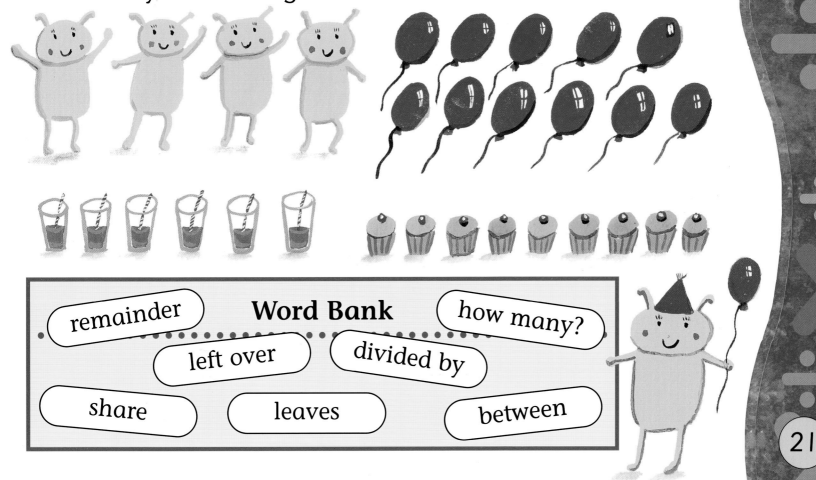

Word Bank

remainder
how many?
left over
divided by
share
leaves
between

Jumping back and dividing

We can use a number track to help with dividing.

Dividing is the same as subtracting the same number lots of times.

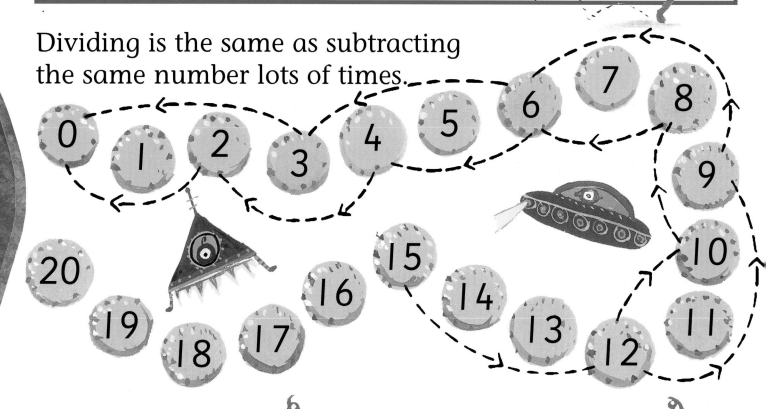

Start on 12.
Make hops of 2 towards zero.
You will make 6 hops.
There are 6 twos in 12.
12 divided by 2 equals 6.

$$12 \div 2 = 6$$

Start on 15.
Make hops of 3 towards zero.
You will make 5 hops.
There are 5 threes in 15.
15 divided by 3 equals 5.

$$15 \div 3 = 5$$

Use the number track to help you with each division.

Look at how far each alien jumps. Start on 20. How many jumps to reach zero? Who will not reach zero?

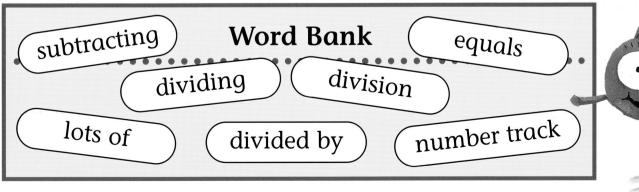

Word Bank

subtracting   equals   dividing   division   lots of   divided by   number track

Rectangle patterns

Rectangle patterns have rows and columns. Rows go across from side to side. Columns go up and down.

In this rectangle pattern each row has 4.
Each column has 3.

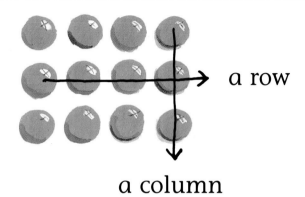

a row

a column

A rectangle pattern for 12.

$$12 = 4 \times 3$$

$$12 = 3 \times 4$$

Here are two more rectangle patterns.

$$20 = 4 \times 5$$

$$20 = 5 \times 4$$

$$12 = 2 \times 6$$

$$12 = 6 \times 2$$

Look at these rectangle patterns.
How many rows in each?
How many columns in each?
How many altogether in each?

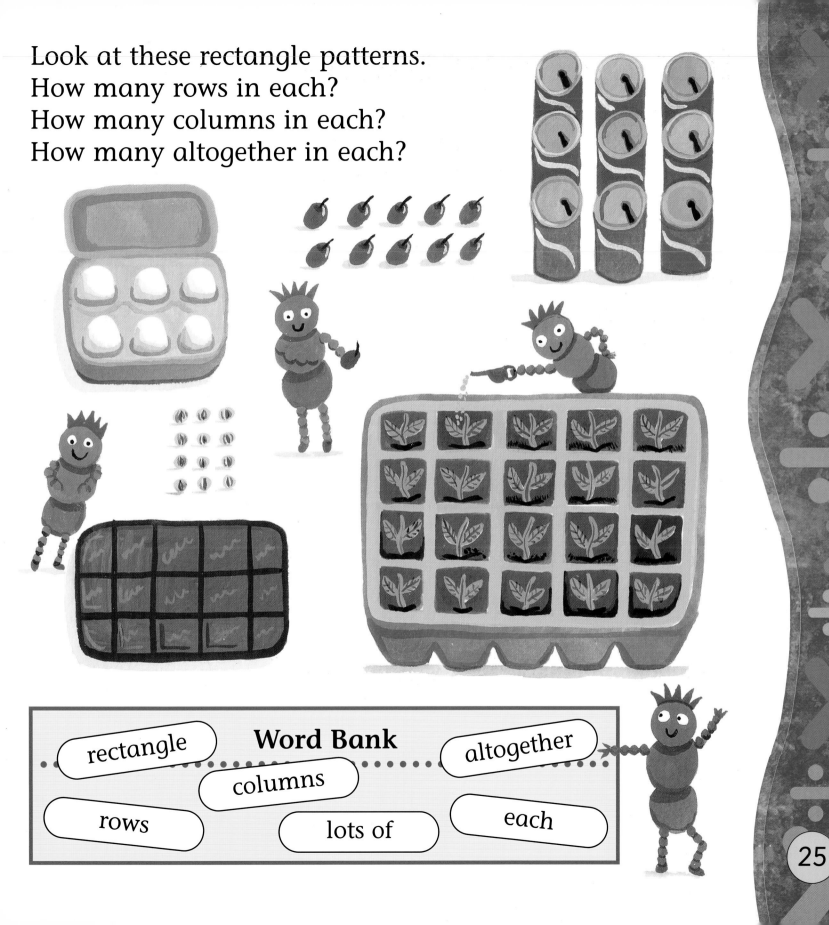

Word Bank

rectangle
columns
rows
altogether
lots of
each

Multiplication tables

Here is how the two times table is made.

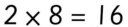

$2 \times 1 = 2$

$2 + 2 = 4$
$2 \times 2 = 4$

$2 + 2 + 2 = 6$
$2 \times 3 = 6$

$2 + 2 + 2 + 2 = 8$
$2 \times 4 = 8$

$2 + 2 + 2 + 2 + 2 = 10$
$2 \times 5 = 10$

$2 + 2 + 2 + 2 + 2 + 2 = 12$
$2 \times 6 = 12$

$2 + 2 + 2 + 2 + 2 + 2 + 2 = 14$
$2 \times 7 = 14$

$2 + 2 + 2 + 2 + 2 + 2 + 2 + 2 = 16$
$2 \times 8 = 16$

$2 + 2 + 2 + 2 + 2 + 2 + 2 + 2 + 2 = 18$
$2 \times 9 = 18$

$2 + 2 + 2 + 2 + 2 + 2 + 2 + 2 + 2 + 2 = 20$
$2 \times 10 = 20$

The other tables are made in the same way.

Here are the multiplication tables for 2, 5, and 10.

2 times table

2 × 0	0 × 2	0
2 × 1	1 × 2	2
2 × 2	2 × 2	4
2 × 3	3 × 2	6
2 × 4	4 × 2	8
2 × 5	5 × 2	10
2 × 6	6 × 2	12
2 × 7	7 × 2	14
2 × 8	8 × 2	16
2 × 9	9 × 2	18
2 × 10	10 × 2	20

5 times table

5 × 0	0 × 5	0
5 × 1	1 × 5	5
5 × 2	2 × 5	10
5 × 3	3 × 5	15
5 × 4	4 × 5	20
5 × 5	5 × 5	25
5 × 6	6 × 5	30
5 × 7	7 × 5	35
5 × 8	8 × 5	40
5 × 9	9 × 5	45
5 × 10	10 × 5	50

10 times table

10 × 0	0 × 10	0
10 × 1	1 × 10	10
10 × 2	2 × 10	20
10 × 3	3 × 10	30
10 × 4	4 × 10	40
10 × 5	5 × 10	50
10 × 6	6 × 10	60
10 × 7	7 × 10	70
10 × 8	8 × 10	80
10 × 9	9 × 10	90
10 × 10	10 × 10	100

Word Bank

doubles

doubled

multiplying

double

twice

6

×2

multiply

twins

multiplication

how many?

times

each

multiplied by

lots of

Word Bank

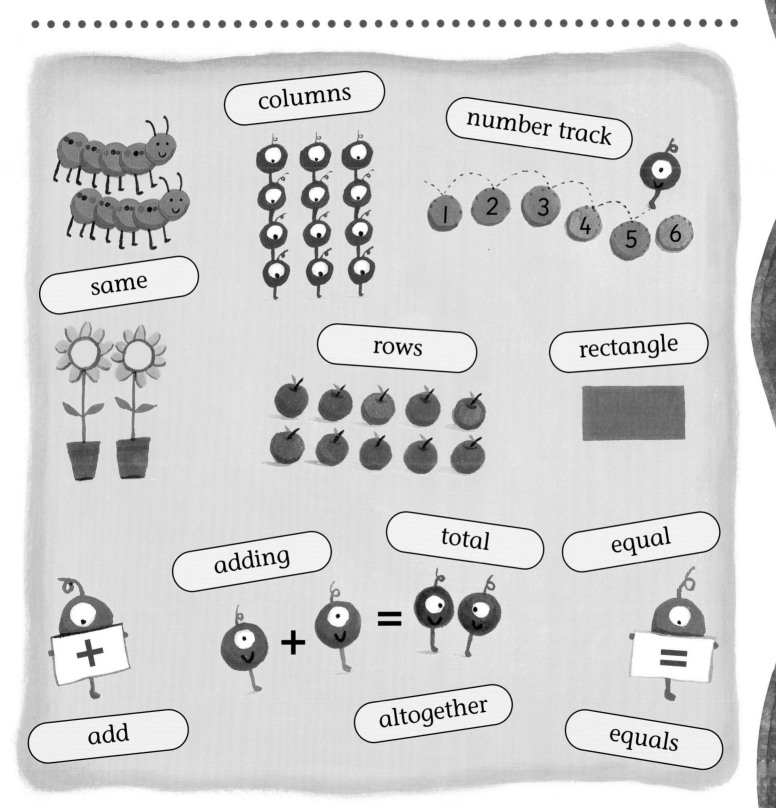

columns

number track

1 2 3 4 5 6

same

rows

rectangle

adding

total

equal

add

altogether

equals

Word Bank

Word Bank

larger

smaller

sharing

between

share

shared by

different

whole

equal parts

leaves

remainder

third

left over

subtracting

fraction

Multiplying and Dividing Quiz

Which number will leave the machine?

Which number will leave the machine?

Which of these pies have been cut into quarters?

How many petals on 4 flowers?

Share these stars between 3 aliens. How many will each get?